Long Rain

Poetry

Lenard D. Moore

Introduction by
Guy Davenport

Wet Cement Press
Berkeley, California

ISBN: 978-1-7324369-9-2

Introduction by Guy Davenport (©1994) used by permission of Erik A. Reece for the Estate of Guy Davenport

Cover image: Japanese kanji for rin'u "a long spell of rain"

Wet Cement Press
Berkeley, California

www.wetcementpress.com

Wet Cement Press publishes small handheld books of poetry, prose and hybrid genius.

WCP10-4

Contents

Introduction   7

   Earth   15
   Wind   43
   Fire   61
   Water   107

About the Author   133
Acknowledgments   135

Introduction[1]

—Guy Davenport

In Japan in the seventh century the emperor Tenji issued an edict through his Minister of the Interior Fujiwara no Kamatari "to debate the merits of the fragrance of thousands of flowers on a spring hill as opposed to the color of hundreds of leaves on an autumn hill" (as Hiroaki Sato and Burton Watson record in their anthology of Japanese poetry, *From the Country of Eight Islands*, to gloss a tanka by the Princess Nukada, who gave springtime its due but chose "the autumn hill").

Psychologists have rarely, if ever, looked at the weather in diagnosing illnesses of the soul, though poets have, from Sappho's springtimes and Alkman's winters to the landscapes that have been the very ground of all American poetry. How shadows lie in

---

[1] An earlier version of this collection was first assembled in 1994. Guy Davenport's introduction was written at that time and is published here for the first time. The tanka poetic form dates from 7th century Japan and is sometimes compared, in spirit, with the English sonnet.

the yard, how light falls through the apple tree, how frost splinters a ploughed field are decisive components of our euphoria or our despair.

Weather has always been a correlative in drama. Tempests and moonlit summer nights, golden autumn days and winter frost have the status of characters in Shakespeare. Thoreau spent his life studying day by day the chemistry of the weather and his soul.

Lenard Moore is a Japanese poet who lives in North Carolina, or a North Carolina poet who lives in an imaginary medieval Japan. He has been a farmer, an American soldier in Germany, a schoolteacher; his ancestors came from Africa in chains. He seems, to the world's eye, to be as representative a husband, father, and citizen as any sociologist might point to as a statistically ordinary well-behaved American. And the sociologist would be wrong, for Lenard Moore is a poet, and all good poets are extraordinary, and very good ones are unique.

In all of his poems Lenard Moore has paid careful attention to the time of day and time of year. In this book he gives up

narrative and anecdote for those sharp observations of moments that we know to be the
soul of classical Japanese poetry. In the West
the Greeks and Romans had the epigram, a
poem of a few lines only, usually four. They
served as inscriptions on monuments and
tombstones, as love poems and bawdy jokes,
and ranged in sentiment from the poignant
to the satiric. Compared to their Japanese
counterpart, they appear earth-bound and
guileless. The Greek poet writes that his
girlfriend Dorothea smells like quinces,
wears neat sandals, and peeps at him shyly
around the door. To the Japanese this would
be indecently straightforward. The quince
alone would have served the Japanese poet,
in a secluded part of a garden.

Lenard Moore is both Japanese and
Western:

> in an instant
> blue jays switch places
> on the powerline
> I listen to its humming
> as the sun goes down

The agility of colorful birds, wind thrumming the power line sunset. The observation could easily be Thoreau's. He was fascinated by the music of telegraph wires. He would have recorded the territorial dance of the blue jays in his journal. He was a connoisseur of sunsets. Wallace Stevens made a meditation of watching a blackbird, and Ezra Pound at Pisa saw birds on power lines as musical notes on a stave.

Lenard Moore's attention is therefore thoroughly American. It is also thoroughly Japanese: the sharp, spare moment's glance (the n's of the first line hopping about like the jays) to alert us to the restless motion of the turning earth and the flow of electricity through wires. Hokusai and Hiroshige delighted in making the real subject of their prints seem accidental and peripheral.

The blue jays have been around for a million or so years, the sun for billions, the power lines for half a century, the poet for a few decades only. He will outlive the blue jays the earth will outlive the power lines and the sun will outlive the earth. At the moment of the poem there are three adjusting movements, the birds changing places, the poet's glance, and the roll of the earth. There are three streaming continuities: time, light, and electricity. If the jays are male and female, they are courting; if male, disputing a territory.

A child might ask why the jays can be on a wire which it is warned never to touch? In North Carolina folklore the jay is chthonic: it is never seen on Fridays, as it is then in the underworld, with messages about us. Unlike as with the cardinal, one may not make a wish on seeing it. It is a raucous bird, like the crow, and belligerent.

From short vowels ("in an instant") to melodiously long ones ("sun goes down") this little poem is like an elegant phrase of music for voice or violin. Of its twenty words only three are from the classical languages (instant, place, line), and these three have been in the language long enough to live down their Latinity.

We feel that the poet has the right words as we feel the right notes in a song. We feel the poem: there is no other way of apprehending it. It has no moral, no message, no occasion except that of its own art. It is, as a statement, idle. It is interesting as leaves on a sidewalk are interesting, or birdsong at twilight, or daffodils in spring wind. Phainomena, the Greeks said: "things that show themselves." Things that are what we call the world, subject to scrutiny but stubbornly unanswerable to it, so that after all these years we cannot distinguish accident from design, and can account for nothing except a few local causes and effects, and are probably wrong about those.

All we can say about phenomena is that they redirect our attention. We know what big phenomena do—the catastrophes—but what about the small, the jays playing on the power line the butterfly on the hydrangea, the owl hooting in the pines? It is because these are innocent and incidental that they claim the poet's attention. They are the evidence that the large life of things is independent of us and beyond our small experience. They return us to tasting existence and savoring its flavor.

Lenard Moore's studies in the significance of the insignificant is an education for our eyes and proof that being observant is an activity of the imagination.

For my siblings:
Jerome, Ron, Angela,
Wanda, Rodney, and Marvin.

For my daughter, Maiisha.
And for Lynn, who gave her to me.

Earth

Great-Grandma Fannie

She stood ironing board-straight, as if she had a basket on her head, born twenty-four years after the Civil War. I am still captivated by her stern, steady ways of working: brown hands gripped the hoe, chopping weeds away from rows and rows of corn and peanuts, a blue apron around her waist, bonnet on her head. She died in 1972. She walked up and down sun-beaten rows, chopped weeds as steady as machines. Her wooden quilting frame took up most of her front room, hands stitching a patchwork. I am fond of unraveling the quilt of this memory. How could I scissor the thread of that time? It remains here.

> forty-five years
> her house falls
> into itself

shoveling all day
where the garden used to be
fresh smell of red earth
I stop to watch the woodpecker
who hammers on the barn

in an instant
blue jays switch places
on the powerline
I listen to its humming
as the sun goes down

washing pink sheets
she bends over the washtub
this sunsplashed morning
and how warm wind scatters
the scent of her perfume

washing a pan
in the broom-swept yard
a black woman at dawn;
she sings "The Negro Anthem"
as maple leaves rustle

a guinea hen pecks
beneath the mulberry tree—
smell of crushed berries;
searching for new eggs
in the increasing dimness

country night
how many bullfrogs telling
where they are
as I walk the soggy earth
that my grandfather once plowed

May midnight—
she turns the light out
and the music on,
suddenly our rapid breaths
are all I hear

manicured course—
a golf cart crosses
the narrow road
a blimp in the bluing sky
over the shopping mall

on the porch
watching you
pick yellow apples
I long to eat
when you return

morning goes:
the blues woman chants
in the summer heat,
while hanging the wash
this end of the clothesline

beachbound at noonday—
the drawbridge opens and
a tugboat passes through;
we wait in the car
until the bridge goes down

at the blueberry farm
white sandy road unwinds
in the shadeless noon
black picker with blue lips drops
handful of berries in a pail

sunless day
a black boy picking apples
all by himself;
listening from the dirt road
the blue jay on the oak stump

a swoop of flies
blackening the dead dog
in the hayfield;
grapes ripening
in the dust

rush hour
a black snake half-coiled
on the highway
the scent of cut grass
lingers all the way

at the beach
the two of us alone
I feel her legs
open wider and wider
in the darkening air

bats fly dizzily
over the roof of my car,
in slow motion;
while rolling the window up,
my heart pounds and pounds

the night is long
a tavern just off the road
with only one car,
but the man and woman hug
to the song on the jukebox

combing her hair
as leaves fall all around us
I finger each silky strand
and how black it remains
after forty years together

dawn light
the widow rakes leaves
from around her porch
now she spies the man
passing on the tractor

I paint my own face
the oval mirror gives back,
and autumn maples
dripping through the bay window,
still I brush stroke the canvas

October night
walking the grove of sweet gums
I startle a cat
and a black shape shimmers
in the curving path

evening chill
a white-haired woman
drinking sassafras tea
the nurse straightens a lithograph
on the pink wall

wintry midnight—
again the distant owl's hoot
on this starry night;
stalking the ancient farmstead
an old fox and another

Groundhog Day:
how the child's shadow
slips into the hole
quietly waiting near the barn
that man with a camera

Wind

In the Owl's Claws

After leaving the D. H. Hill Library at North Carolina State University, I notice the evening deepening all around me. A hint of orange flickers in the colossal trees along both sides of Hillsborough Street. Rainwater dries on the asphalt. Not a single shadow stirs. With hands gripping the steering wheel, I drive toward home, looking skyward. Jazz slips out of the radio. I watch the traffic light. No one else is in the car with me as I continue homeward, ready to settle into my house for the rest of this evening. I am getting hungry. I begin dreaming of hot baked sweet potatoes, barbecued chicken, buttermilk biscuits, okra, and macaroni and cheese. Suddenly I glimpse something gray moving in the sky. Momentarily, the riffs of a saxophone on my car radio seem to turn to silence. Coolness settles all around me. My eyes follow the enormous gray wings punctuating the slowly-darkening sky, studying its calmness while being absorbed in its own moment.

moon on yellow aspens
an owl flies
beyond my windshield

Witnessing a small bird in the owl's claws
makes me feel a sadness for all living
things. It is the uncertainty of how we will
depart from the earth. A few clouds creep
across the face of the moon. It seems as if
that owl wanted me to see him. It is the
way he swooped on the currents of Caroli-
na air. Bonded by the natural world, I am
one with this moment.

late night
remembering the clasped claws
of the owl

open Venetian blinds
moonlight strikes
the *Birds* book

...

quiet before dawn
the salty wind slipping
into the cottage
her black panties drift backwards
on the rusty hanger

budding apple trees;
a red bird still holds his perch
even through these winds...
the noonday sun emerges
high over this old homestead

man with a goatee
hunkers in the onion patch—
the wind lifts,
while I descend the steps
into early light

I sniff the wind
as the scent of honeysuckle
rises from the path
Her blouse blows wide open
the shape of her full breasts

tornado lifts off
the top of the old couple's house—
the sudden quiet
until a burst of birdsong
in all that sunbleached stillness

noon tornado gone—
in the century-old oak
a sunwashed beehive
where silence unfolds to droning
then a gentle wind

just off the highway
small shabby house in the corn patch—
lasting overcast;
dust cloud behind the tractor
as a distant windmill turns

the sand flies
shadowless across the yard
as day cools off
and leaves a choir of crickets
like memory linking me here

breeze off the river...
a tailless dog barks and barks
near the junk heap
my wife and I unlock hands,
gaze beneath mossy willows

morning glories
wrapping around the cornstalks
that rattle and rattle—
then I look straight
into the eyes of a raccoon

two black girls
playing hopscotch
in noon wind
between turns
falling leaves

stranger nearing—
in an angle of sun
the hound's bark
grows deeper
and shapes on the wind

a cloud of breath
emerges from her mouth
no time for kissing
but we walk arm-in-arm
down the narrow path

at the river's edge
only my father hears
the owl that's whitening
as morning wind stirs the limbs
of the longleaf pine in snow

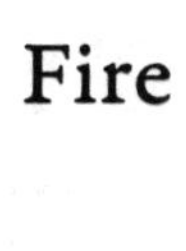

Fire

Cleaning the Attic

Listen, I must tell you this. I can't wait. After today, it will be too late. You realize what memory shaped on this day. Twenty-five years ago, I left for Basic Training. We reunited later that evening. You took me to your mother's house. I remember our kisses, the fire shooting through us. I want to celebrate. Despite the years, I still savor that hot August day. The recruiter drove me to Raleigh, where I found you again. I couldn't forget, let such major events dwindle. I don't need a photograph of that time. I can still see you: chocolate complexion, short black curls, eyes brown and gleaming. Cat eyes testifying love. As if slipping into a dream. We touched like water, whispered like wind. We've got to tell our grown daughter.

> unfolding her letter
> from the dusty trunk—
> twilight breeze

...

spring cleaning—
sound of the vacuum cleaner
from room to room
the sun's sharp ray
shining on the candy dish

noonday sunshine
blazing the greening hills
of this old homestead...
a mild wind pushing
against northward floating geese

seen by white moonlight,
underwear on the clothesline,
flapping in warm wind...
an old bulldog barking
as someone slams the shack door

old photographer
enters the white tulip garden
this dank night
how a streetlight pulses
on the sloping sidewalk

rising sun
the pregnant woman walks
through falling mist
with the fragrance of pine
the ancient path narrows

on the sandbank
a cluster of swallowtails
comes and goes
she and I are so steadfast
as the sun strikes the river

fragrance of old lilacs
across the hospital lawn—
wheelchair in the sun;
beyond the gravel side road
the sea rumples more and more

chips of pinewood
falling off the sunsplashed truck
that turns at the light;
a trail of black exhaust
coming toward my windshield

purple collards
wilting in the noonday sun
on this farm...
blackbirds floating eastward
behind a few distant clouds

glowing moon
shadow comes and goes
through the doorway
she raises her legs
around my neck

red summer sunrise—
a lone old woman sniffing
the wind-tipped roses...
thin white clouds floating
over the distant mountains

shucking sweet corn
on the front porch swing—
the falling light
where crow after crow ascend
into the wood-smoked sky

anniversary
a point of light flickers
on the buffed floor—
our daughter notices it
while cooking breakfast

summer sunburst:
she puts on her sunglasses
and reads the novel;
a towel hangs over
the glinting chair

sun in my side mirror
the rumps of brown horses
shimmer to the right
the sloping fence stretches
mile after sunny mile

my professor and I
talk in the parking lot
stillness all around us
back row of cars glints
inside the high wire fence

full sun
a piece of glass shines
on the sand
while we wax the car
at the country store

endless heat
the old mule barely pulls
a flat sled of hay
now and then the farmer yells
from the bluegreen meadow

stopped at the light—
swarms of gnats hover
around my car;
the sound of water gushes
out of the fire hydrant

idle sun—
a black ant goes back
across the leaflet;
the sound of a chainsaw
breaks through the woodlot

at the cookout
a green fly swerving away
in the hushed light
grass curling around the grill
beside that tent black with crepe

a black man bending
over the low cotton bush—
sunfire on his back;
the flap of a burlap sack
while blues hide in my throat

in the hot field
he hoists a watermelon
out of the shadow—
sweet smell rises from the weeds
and all those ants congregate!

the brush fire in the hills
reminds me
when grandfather's house burned
so fast
the year after boot camp

black-eyed peas and rice
steaming on the chipped blue plate
a spear of sunlight
raking across the iron pot
beside the vase of mums

Funeral Parlor:
a black man rolls the casket
down the crowded aisle,
little by little his shoes
shadow/shine in the white light

late summer
a woman presses another's hair
in the kitchen
inch by inch the sun
reaches the folding chair

flaming clouds
fade in the lake at sunfall—
splash of a bass
then the long silence persists
and beyond: white birds winging

gazing at the stars
that woman
in a black bikini,
how bright her eyes
as the lighthouse flashes

moon over the cottage:
even the curves
of her body
filled with light,
the beads of sweat

whole night sky lights up
by single flash of lightning—
the slickening street;
an old man hunches over
a discarded clothesbasket

heading home—
dozens of planes roaring
in the night sky;
no wind pushing back
the suburban heat

nippy morning—
the hotel worker unfolds
and refolds the rag
sun strokes her sandy hair
as a feather floats by

the hunter coughs—
a band of deer leaping
toward the light;
a bunch of pine needles
falling this windy morning

the evening comes
our bedroom perfectly
full of fall light
how quietly you sleep
as I talk on the phone

autumn wedding—
two men in gloves light candles
as the sun goes dim;
I sit motionless
listening for the bride's song

shattering into shards
my grandma's porcelain vase—
autumn sun goes down
and tangled vines hang over
the plain basin of water

autumn moon rises;
rot of pumpkins rides the breeze
on remnants of fog;
old cabin on a hillside
where hungry wild deer roam

an autumn night—
beside the telephone booth
the old woman waits
she grips her pocketbook
when the shadow moves

alone in the park
suddenly leaf after leaf
falling on the lovers
near a gray granite stone
this starry night

last of winter sun
I adjust the bedroom blinds
for her to undress
I pull back the tightened sheets,
feeling the song in my heart

winter night
the empty house settles
with no sign of stopping—
branches at the window
their shadows on me

the fireplace crackles
in the darkening mirror—
first smell of gumbo;
rhythm of blues tugging at me,
while I sit on my couch alone

Water

Watery Tuesday, April 9, 1968

I remember that ninth day, a learning day: we're lining up at the classroom door. Not knowing what to expect but obeying our fourth-grade teacher. We love our teacher. She's the only white teacher at our school. If we get out of line, she'll say, "Bend over and grab your ankles." We don't want to feel the smack of her tan plastic baseball bat. We love to sing the songs in Spanish and dance in her class. Today we walk single file, the straightest line, to the cafeteria where the glossy wooden stage waits like the black and white TV. We watch Reverend Dr. Martin Luther King, Jr.'s funeral. We weep salt water, keep sobbing until we return to class.

> spring daylight—
> a pot or pan bangs
> behind us

⋯

surging water seeps
through the tall wall of sandbags—
white body of light;
goldenrod on the hillside,
tossing in shifty wind

a woman kneels
where a fountain rises and falls;
a chickadee sings
in the black walnut tree
that towers over me

a note
from the stenographer—
the words
dripping off this paper
with spring rain

honeymoon night—
her gown on the bedpost
as the bedsprings creak
hour after hour spring rain
dripping down the window

off her face
it drips—the warm rain
and the make-up
I clutch her hand
under the loblolly pine

the aged panhandler
in black alligator shoes,
humming in the rain—
how his silent blues
settles into my ears

twelve noon
a green tin lunchbox gleaming
behind the courthouse
goldfish swimming under
water lilies in the pond

fine rain slanting down—
sharecropper blowing his sax
near the post office;
the distant satellite dish
turns toward the clouded sky

morning comes:
an alligator splashes
into murky water
and I stand back
in a pool of light

thick clouds
nailed to the post
a "No Fishing" sign
on the creek's bank
a pile of fish heads

a school of clouds
floating by the jellyfish
barnacles on the rock
between the two docked boats
here and there an osprey's coo

while it softly rains
the sun hides behind a huge cloud
this summer evening
a pack of stray dogs sniffing
the glistening green dumpster

long rain—
a hawk settling
in the dead oak
how the umbrella trembles
in my bony hand

rain ends—
reflection of headlights creeping
down the two-lane road
and from the hushed woods
a black cat crossing my path

the dog laps its face
in the tub of last night's rain—
patch of full sunlight,
golden like the maples
in the backyard

painting a vista
of the autumn day ocean
the rhythm of it
moving in my hand
ghost of a crab

a day without wind—
a fine evening rain hisses
through yellow willows;
the teenager unbraiding
her grandma's thinning gray hair

in winter light
she pours tea from the kettle
and steam rises;
I slice the pink grapefruit,
its juice spills on the table

bright snow:
a four-wheel drive grinds
up the hill
I slip and slide
on my way back home

morning deepens
the balding man scrapes ice
off the Cadillac
while I jog my shepherd
around the subdivision

old black men standing
in front of the corner store
sun soaks their overcoats
and on the sidewalk
a gathering of shadows

late winter
the widow works the dough
for bread
and the heat rises
from the oven

I caress her lips
at the kitchen table—
the sound of rain
deepens against my heart
this winter night

About the Author

Lenard D. Moore is an internationally acclaimed poet and anthologist, especially known for his work with haiku and other Japanese forms. His work has been published in more than sixteen countries and translated into more than twelve languages. Moore is the author of *The Geography Of Jazz, A Temple Looming, Desert Storm: A Brief History, Forever Home,* and *The Open Eye* among other books. He is also the editor of *All The Songs We Sing* and *One Window's Light: A Collection of Haiku,* (winner of the Haiku Society of America 2018 Merit Book Award). He has taught creative writing and African American literature and has collaborated with poets, visual artists, musicians and dancers on several projects. He is the founder and executive director of the Carolina African American Writers' Collective, and co-founder of the Washington Street Writers Group. He was the first African American President of the Haiku Society of America, and is the Executive Chairman of the North Carolina Haiku Society. Among his numerous awards are the North Carolina Award for Literature, Furious Flower Laureate Ring, Haiku Museum of Tokyo Award, Margaret Walker Creative Writing Award, Indies Arts Award, and Cave Canem Fellowships. He is a U.S. Army veteran, who earned his Master of Arts in English and African American Literature from North Carolina Agricultural and Technical State University and his Bachelor of Arts in Liberal Studies with a minor in English (Magna Cum Laude) from Shaw University.

Acknowledgments

Grateful acknowledgment is made to the editors of the following magazines where some of these poems were first published, some in different versions: *Black American Literature Forum, Black Bough, Black Buzzard Review, Blue Buildings, Blue Unicorn, Brussels Sprout, Cicada, Contemporary Haibun Online, Dragonfly, Electrum, Five Lines Down, The Griot, Hummingbird, Japanophile, Journeys, Lynx, Mirrors, Northwest Literary Forum, Pembroke Magazine, The Piedmont Literary Review, Point Judith Light, Prophetic Voices, The Tanka Journal, Voices International* and *Xavier Review.* Grateful acknowledgment is also made to the editors of the following anthologies in which some of these poems also appeared: *The Tanka Anthology* (Red Moon Press), *Tanka Splendor* 1994 (AHA Books), *Wind Five Folded* (AHA Books). The author would also like to thank the editors at Wet Cement Press for their support of this book.